Phoenix Ashes

Amber Rodgers

BookLeaf Publishing

Presentation by *BookLeaf Publishing*

Web: www.bookleafpub.com

E-mail: info@bookleafpub.com

ISBN: 9789357615952

First edition 2022

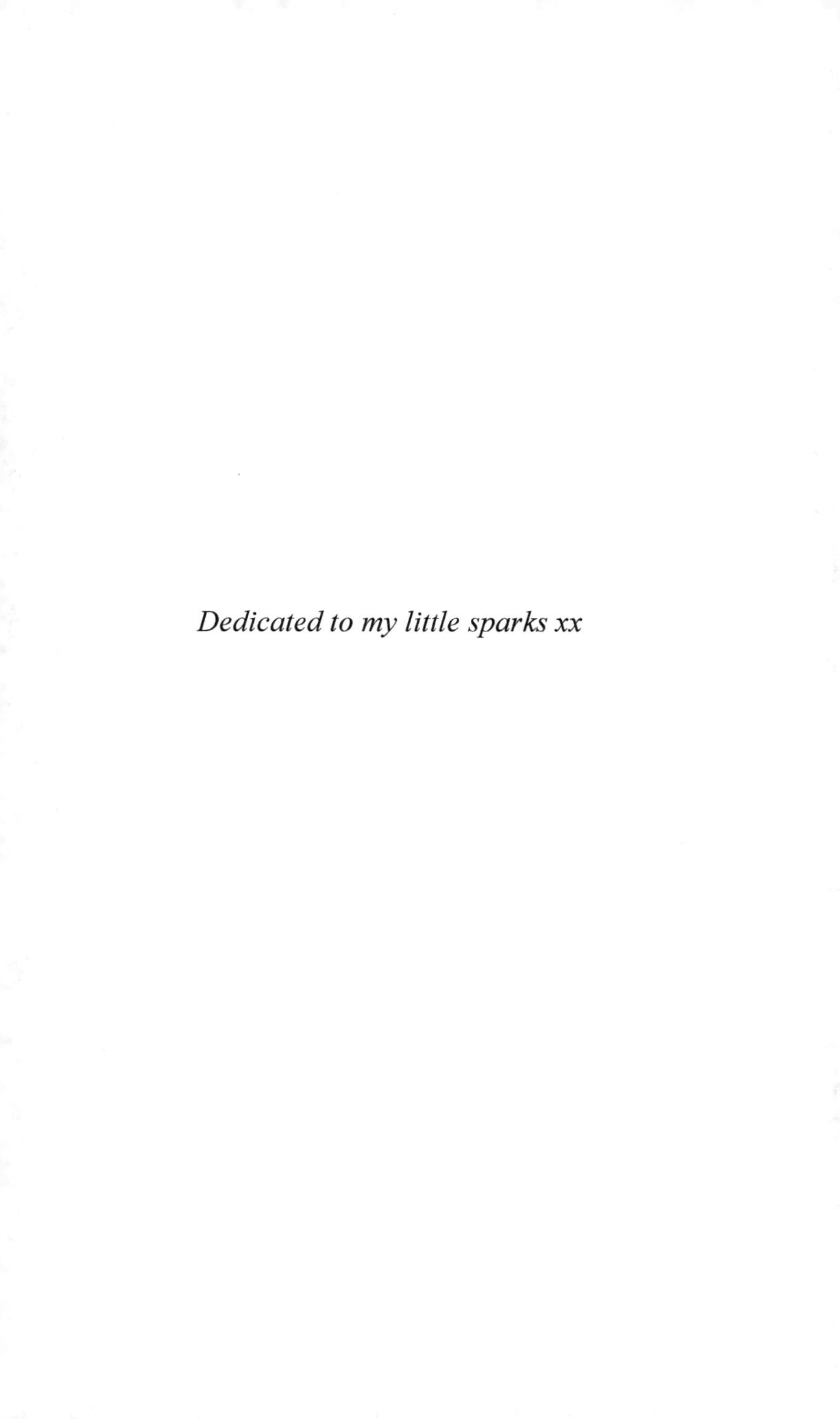

Dedicated to my little sparks xx

ACKNOWLEDGEMENT

I want to thank my mum and dad for supporting me and treating my children as their own. I want to thank my sister and her husband for always looking out for my children and making them feel loved.

I also want to thank my grandparents, Nan and Pop, for making myself and my boys feel like we always have a place to go!

PREFACE

This collection of poems is a personal reflection of experiences myself and my family have faced. These experiences came to a head when we tragically lost our possessions in a house fire in September 2022.

This house fire helped me realise that fire can bring so much new growth and help start fresh - out with the old, in with the new. This house fire inspired me to begin reflecting on my past experiences with coercive family violence, as well as my journey into single parenthood and all that revolves around that.

The image of the phoenix perfectly encapsulates what I want to achieve and what I want for myself and my children. I am the phoenix coming from the ashes, anew, a whole, and a ready version of myself.

Fire

1

Bright,
Pure,
Ferocious,
It moved like a snake.
Creeping through the walls,
Snaking along the wires.
The windows exploded,
The clothing tattered.
And standing within the devastation,
A lone figure.
She is risen.

Ashes

What was left?
What could survive such an inferno?
Skin was peeling,
Blisters bursting in the new light.

No blood pooled below her feet.
No soot marred her skin.
No evidence of flame,
Other than her peeling flesh.
No muscle or bone showed through,
New skin.

New skin from ashes.

Sparks

Two small sparks burst beside her.
Burning,
Fluttering,
Never slowing to match her.
No need for explosion,
No need for ashes.
Two simple flames,
Flames that will never be doused.
Never see water,
Never touch rain.
Two small flames,
Will burn their own path.
A path of their own,
A path full of their potential.
A path blazed without prejudice,
A path blazed behind the phoenix.
The Phoenix will never douse their flames,
The Phoenix will never deny their hunger.
The Phoenix will guide their path,
And lead them to Paradise.

Smoke

Messages from smoke,
Can you read them?
Messages from smoke,
Can you decipher?
Messages delivered through flame and burning,
Will you heed the call?
The calling of smoke to signal what's happened,
The calling of smoke to signal the burning.
The smoke to cover the sky,
To cover the sun,
To cover the driveway.
The smoke to cover the pain.
What pain?
The pain is covered,
Waiting for a chance to rear its head.
Rear its head when the time doesn't call,
When the opportunity isn't present.
Read its head when she is most vulnerable.
The smoke hides the pain,
She'll feel it eventually.

Five Hundred Years

5

The ashes represent the time before,
The fire represents a new beginning.
The new beginning that leaves the old behind,
The behind may be a part of the new.
Five Hundred Years makes an impact,
Five hundred years isn't easily left behind.
Hidden suffering
Hidden pain.
Hidden gems to be fired,
Fired for their new purpose.

Cracks

Before the explosion,
Before the fire,
Before the smoke,
Before the ashes,
There was a broken jar.

A cracked jar that bled its contents,
A cracked jar that leaked upon everyone's touch.
A cracked jar that believed healing was never
coming.
Cracks that deepened with each word,
Cracks that shaped the contents until nothing
was able to be held.

Jagged pieces held together with stubbornness
and sheer will.
No glue could fix this,
No tape could hold together what was broken.
No hands could fix these broken pieces.

Hands of flame appeared,
A potter of heat and sparks.
Reshaping was coming,
Rebirth was on its way.
A phoenix was rising.

Ró-gheal

Ró-gheal.
My fire is too bright,
It needs to be turned down.
My fire is too bright,
I need to water it down.
My light is too bright,
I need to hide it away.

Paisean.
My passion will not be hidden.
My passion will not be watered down.
My fire should burn bright.

If my fire is too bright,
You need to hide away.
If my passion is too much,
You need to walk away.
If my fire is too hot,
You need to control yourself.

My tine,
My paisean,
My saol,
My rialacha.

Docile

Don't ever water yourself down.
Your fire,
Your passion,
They were made to burn bright.

Don't ever water yourself down.
Even if they tell you to,
Even if they force you to.
They are the ones that need to reconsider.

Your fire is not theirs.
To control your fire means they win,
Do not let them win.
You control your own fire.

Burn those bridges,
Let the light guide your way.
Do not become docile,
Not for their sake.

You are not here to make them comfortable,
You are not here to be a bystander.
You are here,
You are here to wage war.
You are here to push against the restraints,

And take your seat at the table.

The table built for you.

сядьте на своє місце

Take your seat,
The seat you deserve.
The seat that was waiting for the fire,
The seat that was made for you.

Take your seat,
At the table that wants you to fail.
At the table that mourns your past self.

Take your seat at the table.
The table that you control,
Control with boundaries,
Control with passion and flame.

The table made from Australian Buloke,
The wood that will not crack.
The wood that was hand carved by the women
before you,
Finished in the flame of resurrection.

Take your seat for all the ones before you.
Take your seat for all the ones after you.
Take your seat at the table for those that had to
kneel.

Take your seat at the table for those that fell
silent to the grave.
Take your seat at the table for the forgotten and
abandoned.
Take your seat at the table for the next
generation you will raise.

Alleenstaande Moeder

A fire doused with water
No longer burns.
Instead,
Grey smoke rises.

The water is not water,
Not in this case.
The water is words,
Words that squash a flame.
Words that cause a candle to flicker,
To tremor.
Words that destroy,
Destruction can lead to flame.

The water missed the small sparks,
The sparks the fire had released.
The sparks that were shielded behind their
mother.
The mother,
The once bright flame,
Now grey smoke,
A memory of the flame.

The flame that created them,
The flame that protected them,

The flame that gave them life!

The sparks do not leave their mother's smoky
haze.
With every kiss of their flame,
The water steams above.

The steam making way for something truly
amazing.

A Battered Woman

Words.
Words are weapons.
Words cut like knives,
Divide marrow from bone,
Rewire chemicals,
Poison organs.

Words are weapons.
Tongue like a sword,
No longer a loving caress.
Biting to draw blood and inflict pain.

No pleasure in words anymore.
No joy being showered upon her.
Only fear and pressure.
Not pressure that creates diamonds,
Pressure that squashes her windpipe.

Punches are no longer feared,
They leave their mark.
Words leave scars no one can see,
Scars that she only knows.

Shield of Strength

Sit,
Kneel,
Walk,
Stand.

Sit in who you are.
Who are you?
You are a Phoenix rising,
Rising from ashes,
Rising into victory.

Kneel into who you are.
You are the victor.
You are the Rising,
The reckoning.

Walk in your second coming.
Your new birth,
A new beginning to conquer,
Already conquered.

Stand in the victory.
The victory of overcoming,
The victory of refinement.
You are victorious.

Refiner

Consume me,
And refine me with fire.
Phoenix fire burns,
It reshapes.

You are a new creation.
You have risen above the ashes of your past self.
The ashes of pain and suffering,
The ashes of remorse, shame, and abuse.

You are the Phoenix.
You are the fire.

Sparks II

Two small sparks thrive on your love.
Your protection to thrive.
The phoenix and her feathers,
Shading sparks from rain,
Sheltering sparks from wind.

These sparks are your legacy.
These sparks are your beginning.
Your life continues in these sparks,
Your life is for these sparks.

These sparks are yours.
Yours to love,
Yours to nurture,
Yours to guide.

These sparks will change the world.
Your guidance will change their world.

Ceartais

Ceartais,
Justice.
A strange word for a Phoenix to hold on to.

Ceartais,
Justice.
The burning provides justice.
A new chance to rise.

A rising above,
Above the problems that seek to destroy,
Above the people that push boundaries.

Boundaries in place to protect sparks.
Protecting sparks is the Phoenix's life.

Vervulling

Fulfilled.
Is the Phoenix fulfilled?
What dreams does the Phoenix have?
What does the Phoenix strive for?

Her sparks.
The sparks are her only life.
Her life with fulfilment.
Vervulling,
The fulfilment for her sparks.

The space,
The simple life,
Away from the race of life.
The race of life that dulls sparks,
Sparks like hers.

Her fulfilment comes when her sparks live their
life free from rain.

Dúnadh

Do you seek dúnadh?
Seeking that which needs to be done.
That which needs to be seen to be done with.

The seeing,
The witnessing,
The ogling of ashes.
Ashes that will float on the wind.

Ashes on the wind,
No need for closure.
The Phoenix has no time for closure.

Føniks

21

Aske av smerte,
Asken av lidelse.
Knuste drømmer,
Glemte lidenskaper.

Ashes of pain,
Ashes of suffering.
Broken dreams,
Forgotten passions.

Utbrudd av flamme,
Blasting walls from houses.
Aske til aske,
Støv til støv.

The Phoenix rises from the grave,
The grave of her old self.

Life after Fire

The sparks still have their Phoenix,
The Phoenix still has her sparks.

Is home a place?
Home is a feeling.
A feeling of safe,
A feeling of love,
A feeling of warm.

This home is full.
Full of love,
Full of safe,
Full of warm.

The roads have been rocky,
From flame to ashes,
Long and narrow roads are less travelled.

Rest

The Phoenix rests.
Her flame was not her restful end.
Her flame was the beginning,
The pain that starts a new season.
The ice that melts,
From Winter to Spring.

The Phoenix rests.
Rest is Important.
The Phoenix models self care.
Her sparks learn from her.
Her example nourishes them.

The Winter brings dormancy,
Allows plants to have their rest.
The Spring brings life,
Springs bulbs and seeds into explosions of
colour.

The Phoenix melted the ice of her world,
The ice that kept her cold,
The ice that kept her hidden.
The water steamed above,
Causing clouds of heat.

The Phoenix rose,
The Phoenix now rests.

Sparks III

Her sparks walk their path,
Guided by a fiery wing.
The wing does not feel their heat,
It mirrors her own.

For so long she lived in the dark
Hiding her flame to please others.
For so long she stayed in the shadows
Avoiding the contact from those that sought to
devour her.
Without her flame,
The wolves found her,
Ripped her insides apart.
Devoured her innocence.

Her sparks will not know that pain.
Her sparks will not know dulling their flame.
Their flame will be their guiding light,
A light for the reckoning.
A light to stave off darkness,
For it cannot be extinguished.

Not under the Phoenix's watch.